WHERE HOPE COMES FROM

WHERE HOPE COMES FROM

Poems of Resilience, Healing, and Light

NIKITA GILL

New York

Hachette Books
Hachette Book Group
1290 Avenue of the Americas
New York, NY 10104
HachetteBooks.com
Twitter.com/HachetteBooks
Instagram.com/HachetteBooks

Originally published in Great Britain in 2021 by Trapeze, an imprint of The Orion Publishing Group Ltd.

First Hachette Books Edition: June 2021

Published by Hachette Books, an imprint of Perseus Books, LLC, a subsidiary of Hachette Book Group, Inc. The Hachette Books name and logo is a trademark of the Hachette Book Group.

The Hachette Speakers Bureau provides a wide range of authors for speaking events.

To find out more, go to www.hachettespeakersbureau.com or call (866) 376-6591.

The publisher is not responsible for websites (or their content) that are not owned by the publisher.

Library of Congress Control Number: 2021934392

ISBNs: 978-0-306-82640-5 (trade paperback), 978-0-306-82641-2 (ebook)

Printed in the United States of America

LSC-C

Printing 2, 2023

For you,
who needs
to believe again.

A Note

In the year 2020, a devastating pandemic has wreaked havoc on our lives. No human has been left untouched by the devastation and the chaos that coronavirus has brought, and in this feeling of uncertainty we are united. I am writing to you from the past. Still in the middle of this pandemic, I was told that I was high-risk; I was thousands of miles away from my loved ones, worry for them consuming my every waking moment; I have found myself more alone than I have ever felt before.

And then…people we loved started dying and we could not say goodbye. All of this while we were living in one of the most politically polarized and divisive times in living history—peaceful protests for racial justice, fighting against racism and police brutality, were willfully misconstrued by people to suit their own political agendas, causing further chaos in a heartbreaking time.

All sources of hope now shattered, I realized that this was the year I had to rebuild hope from scratch, and to do that I needed to find the source. The good thing about loneliness is that it holds more answers than the warmth and chatter in crowded places that offer kind distractions do. So I did what I knew best. I wrote poems, mantras, affirmations, reasons to live. I learned how to honor despair so I could make way for happiness. And I also realized that I was not alone in this deep chasm of sadness. So many people were there with me. Perhaps even you.

We may not know each other. We may never meet. But if you chance upon this book, I want you to know that no matter what you are going through, no matter how big and deep and painful those feelings are, you are not alone. You do not walk this earth, feet blistered with burdens and suffering, by yourself. There are so many of us who walk with you, yet each one of us believes we are abandoned in our pain. Perhaps this is because we are always looking ahead. The next hurdle, the next part of the journey, the future. Or looking behind, unable to see any future because we are living in the past. It's strange how we never turn our heads to the side. If we did, we would realize that we are not alone, even in self-isolation, especially through a pandemic. The beauty of our species comes from our togetherness. We are campfire tales, parental wisdom, grandmothers' accounts, fables of friendships and conversations in the dark and in the pale light of morning. The truth of us is in the words, "I see you," when you see someone struggling.

We are the sum total of our stories in the end, the ones we share by colliding with each other. Where love, sadness, anger, and truth all come alive because we met and imagined together awhile. Stories are where hope comes from, too. We see it reflected in each other every day. When we go above and beyond for one another as volunteers during a pandemic, or when we simply check up on our neighbors and ensure the elderly have everything they need, this kindness, this compassion, this is where hope comes from. But it also comes from standing together against evil. It comes from chaos—rediscovery of truth, understanding loneliness and self-compassion, too.

Hope is an actionable thing, and just like recovery from grief, it is a journey to find hope, too. During my time alone, I turned to my oldest friend—the night sky—to do this. In exploring the life of the stars, I found what I was looking for. Just as there are five stages of grief, there are also five stages of hope. We are going to explore these through the rebirth of a star.

So hold on tight. We are going to do the impossible together and bring a star back to life.

And a Message from the Universe

In every moment of your existence,
several realities
are bursting across the cosmos.

Planets explode.
Stars burst.
Solar systems dissolve

or welcome a new planet
into the orbit of their own
sun-like star.

The universe gives them life
and says,
Now help me live.

Listen.
I am saying
that if you change your thoughts,

you, too, can change your universe.

Black Hole (Despair)
noun

- ASTRONOMY
  A region of space having a gravitational field so intense that no matter or radiation can escape.

- INFORMAL
  A place where lost items go never to be found again.

Reminders to Hold On to in Despair

1. Even at your loneliest, there is someone in this world feeling exactly what you are. There is comfort in this, if you let it in.
2. When you find yourself empty of love, remember that you are 70 percent water. Who do you carry all those lakes and oceans in you for if not to nourish yourself, your own thirsts?
3. There are still people who love you, even if you cannot see them right now.
4. If you must learn to practice something in this time, let it be mercy toward yourself.
5. Survival is ugly on most days. The thing is, you survived. That is all that matters.
6. When time feels strange and non-existent, remember that we learn so much about ourselves in the silence, for if we truly listen, we can hear our ancestors' voices in the crackle of the stars.
7. You are not weak in sickness. You are fighting harder than you ever have before, and this makes you a warrior.
8. What we do not know can fill up a hundred libraries, but here is what we do know: kindness fills the world with only beauty, and tenderness is how flowers grow.

Depression Will Tell You

That the world is ending. It will also tell you how you still have things to do, as yet. For instance, your boss still wants that report emailed to him this morning. No, he doesn't care that you need to be with your family because you are afraid, he needs it *now*. Depression reminds you that your family is probably scared, too. It tells you, they miss you, but you won't be able to spend time with them because you might get fired if you do. And then how will you provide for them. You think of packing a bag, taking your family, and running away. The forest will have you; the trees are safer harbor—they give both shelter and fruit. Anxiety tells you this is a bad idea because you have no survivalist skills. You tell anxiety you have survived it and depression for a while now.

Still, you get to work. Look at the picture of your children. Tell yourself this is for them. Do the best you can. Trust that the best of you is the most of you and even on the days you do not feel it, it is enough. Even now, at the end of the world, with each painful day. It is enough.

It's 2020

And everyone I know is on the verge
of breaking down.
Or has broken down.
Or has felt more tragedies

than the cosmos truly intends
for a person to feel.
And it's hard to say,
This, too, shall pass,

because we don't know if it will.
None of the clichés work.
Not while the world
stands still.

All we can do is pray.
All we can do is not blame each other.
And wish we had enjoyed one another
a little longer the last time we were together.

What is left but
to promise that when we next meet,
we will be kinder.
And fight for a better future together.

After You Died, My Grandmother Told Me

When I say Feel the grief
in full, I mean,
let it break your heart.

How else will it learn
to soften you
to the wounds of others?

Besides, she asks,
how do you think
the ache finally leaves?

No Accidents

He tells me, I *wish I didn't exist*, and he is only nine.
My mouth runs drier than the cracked ground left in
    a once-lake,
and I ask him the necessary, pleading, *why.*

A slip of a child, shy and sweet, who loves silence and
    listening.
He shuffles his feet and looks down on the ground.
I *feel like a mistake. Like I don't matter.*

I do not tell him, *But you have so much to live for.*
I do not tell him, *But if you disappear, we will be sad.*
I do not tell him, *Love will heal you one day.*

Instead I say, *We sit at the edge of a magical ocean so wide,*
we can only use light years to measure it, and every morning,
the sun still rises on you and I and everyone we know.

And every night, the sun disappears to let the moon glow,
and the night sky embraces us with her starry cloak.
Which is to say that the universe has not failed us yet.

Which is also to say, none of this is an accident.
So you, too, must be crafted by the same cosmic hands.
You are no mistake, nothing about you is graceless.

That is the measure of a human life to the cosmos.
So unmeasurable, you are nothing less than a celebration.
All you must do is find your path, move to your destination.

Daily Mantra 1

When the universe could not find
something to live for,
it invented the galaxies and planets
and everything in between.

If you cannot find
something to believe in,
perhaps it is because
you haven't invented it yet.

And the News Says

We all need to become islands
after a lifetime of being told not to.

If we love, we must love from a distance,
the way grief has taught us to.

So we find solace in digital arms instead.
Shining screens instead of shining faces,

longer phone calls, fingers typing,
I *love you* I *miss you* I *need you.*

We pray for our doctors, our nurses,
all our caregivers, and try

to display the best of human nature.
We pretend happy as best we can,

even when everything feels damned,
because this is what it means to be human.

To put on a smiling face and adjust
to the new normal bravely,

say gratefully, I'm *fortunate. All I must do*
is my best to adapt to the lonely.

When truly we mean,
I'd *give this whole island-self up for a hug*

from my best friend,
my brother, my mother.

The Answer

(For J, *who asked how to hide despair*)

This year more than most,

I have searched for
a way to hide despair.
In words, in love,

inside a tree's wizened bark,
under a stone by the ocean,
within a once-sacred temple,

and still,
    it follows
        everywhere.

When the grief begins
to overwhelm me,
I ask the sky for relief.

The sky smiles,
and gives me
two storm songs.

One tells me,
you do not have
to be ashamed of your sadness.

The other says,
you must only know to name it
when it knocks on your heart's door.

Plague Year

As the plague swept across England,
Shakespeare carefully crafted the majesty of King Lear,
the misery of Macbeth, and the tragedy
of Antony and Cleopatra before year's end.

The determination to create immortal work
also found Isaac Newton sequestered in his room
playing rainbows across his walls with prisms,
creating cosmic theories using apple trees.

And the muse still sat on the shoulder
of Edvard Munch during the Spanish Flu, his body riddled
    with disease,
and yet his self-portraits captured more than his gaunt face,
they showed his burning urge to stay alive to paint another
    masterpiece.

Yet to me, no inspiration finds its way.
Instead I look more often out my window to the roads,
to an empty horizon of street lights
in the summer of a Saturday night.

It is a small act of protest,
just to be here and still alive.
This, too, is worthy living.
And it will do just fine.

On My Government-Mandated Walk

I saw that the pub we love
now has a *For Sale* sign in the window.

No bright lights
or warm fireplace.

You'll be glad to know, though,
the mismatched armchairs are gone, too.

I know how much they bothered you.
Inside is now an empty, eerie building.

Once full of life
and now nothing.

I worry about Lou who manned the bar,
always a smile for everyone.

I worry that Charlie and Mary
may not be able to find other jobs.

So this is what happens
to buildings once they lose their people.

The same as what happens to people
when they lose the ones they love.

They become ghostly things,
monuments of memory,

as do all possessions and people
that once upon a time knew such deep, life-giving love.

Stay

It's always on the tip of my tongue.
I sprinkle it in thought at the end
of every sentence I trade with you.

Have you eaten today? *Please stay.*
What do you miss most? *Please stay.*
We'll go for a picnic one day. *Please stay.*

Did I tell you that stars can survive
for millennia without meeting other stars?
Please stay.

Have you got enough medication? *Please stay.*
We are all just water and stardust anyway.
Please stay.

If I promise you a day at the beach,
will you promise me
you will be safe?

Promise me you will not turn
into tendrils of smoke and ash
and memory.

Promise me you will be alive at the end of this
so we can tell our grandchildren
these stories.

Please stay.
Please stay.
Please stay.

The Truth Is...

George Floyd believed in second chances
and community and his daughter's smile.

Elijah McClain had the gentlest heart
and played violin to soothe stray cats.

Breonna Taylor spent her days and nights
helping other people hold on to their lives.

What they deserved is what all humans deserve.
A full life. More gentle greetings from the neighbors

as they leave for work in the mornings.
More family dinners filled with laughter and joy.

More affection and arguments with their lovers.
Warm arms to hold them when they are sad.

New things to learn about love and the soul.
More victories that bring them glory and lessons

from life's defeats. Future friends to celebrate with.
More people to be proud of and who are proud of them.

A chance.
To grow and to love.

A chance.
To find peace.

My Grandmother and I Are Talking About Death Again

Over the phone, her voice feels
even further than the thousands of miles

between us. We talk every Saturday,
but time has lost its meaning during the plague.

She says endings are sacred.
I tell her that they are painful.

Her voice is steady,
For endings to evolve us,

they must be painful.
She says death is faithful. It follows us

from the moment we are born
till we finally learn to welcome it.

When she speaks like this,
I feel like a maze of frozen streets.

An aimless wandering.
Stricken by even the idea

of a world without her in it.
And here we are again, talking about death.

I grip the phone and tell her
she is the only holy I know.

How she must promise me
that, no matter what,

we will see each other again.
That we will always see each other again.

I picture her smile through the phone,
lace tablecloth under careworn, gentle fingers,

the phone shaking against her ear.
One day you must learn

that the god you are seeking
will always live in the act of letting go.

I Wonder What They Would Put in a Museum for Our Times

Masks. The fear of them. The words of the people who called them safety, and the cries of the people who named them muzzles. Photos of empty cities and of fiery protests. The callousness of politicians who did not care. The helplessness of the people who did but could not make a difference. The doctors and nurses who gave their lives fighting for their patients. The trauma of those who had to die alone. The families who had to say goodbye to their loved ones over the phone. The shock that we could not even attend their funerals because that was how the virus spread. The devastation that we could not even bury our dead. Walls upon walls dedicated to the thousands of names sealed forever in time. A promise to protect the legacies they leave behind. The burning words, *Your Death Will Not Be in Vain* and *Never Forget*. The oaths taken that there is more to live for and to fight for yet.

After the First Death

You learn you cannot say goodbye.
That you cannot bury them,
for the illness spreads when people collect.
Even funerals are not exempt.
But mourning, like living, is a verb,
no matter how lonely.

They tell you losing people is hard,
but they neglect to say,
Can you cope with it, truly,
when the world itself is lost?
How endings within endings
are never easy.

When the anguish comes to stay,
it haunts the whole bedroom
and then the house.
It is so heavy, so consuming,
that we have no choice but to turn it into stories
to keep the memories strong.

After all, who else will become
the keeper of their tales
other than your wounded mouth?
Part of you may die with them,
but the stories will stay
to help you live.

From Everything Broken

There is nothing beautiful
about the wreckage
of a human being.

There is nothing pretty
about damage, about pain,
about heartache.

Yet still, despite the ruin,
they show an ocean of courage
when they pick through the debris of their life

to build something beautiful, brand new,
against every odd
that is stacked against them.

And there is no denying
that this,
this is exquisite.

Two Texts for Those I Let Go

(To *the ex-best friend*)

I know this may mean little, coming from me,
but from one small human to another,
I want you to know that love
felt this deeply, this fully, is never lost.

We did not come into the art of this
just to lose ourselves.

We came to turn our bodies
into beacons of hope,
forever calling to each other
in a language only we understand.

It is the end of the world.
I hope you let the sunlight in for longer these days.

(To *the person named Destruction*)

People forget that their actions
not only have consequences,
but victims and witnesses.

People who will carry what you said
or did within their bone marrow,
your disrespect in their sinews.

You are chaos theory:
a butterfly who caused a hurricane
for which you refuse to take responsibility.

There is no goodness in that.
Still, I hope you are safe and warm
and happy wherever you are.

Supernova (Reflection)
noun

- ASTRONOMY
  A star that suddenly increases greatly in brightness because of a catastrophic explosion that ejects most of its mass.

- INFORMAL
  The moment just before death, when a star shines its very brightest.

Reasons to Live Through the Apocalypse

Sunrises. People you have still to meet and laugh with. Songs about love, peace, anger, and revolution. Walks in the woods. The smile you exchange with a stranger when you experience beauty accidentally together. Butterflies. Seeing your grandparents again. The moon in all her forms, whether half or full. Dogs. Birthdays and half-birthdays. That feeling of floating in love. Watching birds eat from bird feeders. The waves of happiness that follow the end of sadness. Brown eyes. Watching a boat cross an empty sea. Sunsets. Dipping your feet in the river. Balconies. Cake. The wind in your face when you roll the car window down on an open highway. Falling asleep to the sound of a steady heartbeat. Warm cups of tea on cold days. Hugs. Night skies. Art museums. Books filled with everything you do not yet know. Long conversations. Long-lost friends. Poetry.

In Self-Quarantine, Watching My Cat from My Bedroom Window

I hope one day I become
as gifted at recognizing
love as my cat is.

I named him after the poet
with the darkest, largest heart
and I think of ravens

every time I call his name.
He is not obedient,
but I would not want him tame.

His tightly coiled body as he stalks birds,
his discerning look when he hears
his name but does not wish to come home.

I, too, hope to be that confident in a love.
Someone who I know will still love me,
even if I do not run to them

every time they call.

Hindsight

All because everything is forbidden now,
I want to go up to the top of the Eiffel Tower
and sing at the top of my lungs.

I want to visit every museum and gallery
I have put off visiting
because work got in the way.

I want to touch the walls
of cathedrals and temples
in fervent prayer.

I want to jump in the ocean
and not even care about my fear of sharks
because viruses kill more people than sharks ever could.

I want to tell everyone
I was too afraid to love that, truly,
I do love them.

Hug them tighter.
Stop time so I can enjoy each kiss longer.
Be more reckless.

Dream bigger.
Chase storms.
Befriend strangers.

Fight less often.
Love a little harder.
See falls for what they are,

a place from which you can only go higher.
See failure for what it is,
just another chance to be a better learner.

Every argument
as a chance to be a better listener.
Breathe in all the sweet air deeper.

All of this resolution is too late because
I did not appreciate life's magic
when it was in my hands.

All this resolution now—
that I will hold on to till the air is safe
to breathe freely again.

Daily Mantra 2

There is still room for love.
Even after being uprooted
or when survival is painful.
Even through trauma.

Just ask the universe
when it aches too much to see,
it will tell you how the big bang
was when everything broke so it could be.

Letter to My Younger Self in Times of Turbulence

Love yourself dangerously. In all the places no one else dares to love you. Fulfill this yearning for yourself. The primal love you hold within your stormskin commands you. All the deep sadnesses made of words and wounds are no match for the pain of a broken heart. From within your own muscle and sinew, you can do this. You can do this—you hold the secret to surviving within your solitude. Fill journals, make art, make beautiful things just for yourself. It doesn't matter what anyone else thinks of them, all that matters is what you think of your own vulnerability. Smile at the skies. You are still here; you are still alive.

And when the thoughts of mortality come to haunt you, think of how nothing is eternal. Everything else accepts it. The gentle robin at your window and even the fearsome tiger in the wild. And if they accept not being eternal, so should you. Your mortality, after all, is the beauty of you. To burn brighter than the sun if only for a matter of seconds to the universe, you are the chrysalis and butterfly, the ember and the wildfire, the story and its ending. Embrace that, embrace it, because this is all you have. This is all we all have. A chance to make something beautiful.

When you feel death has your name on it, tell it to wait another day. You still have so much more to do. Then live, live the way you have never lived before, whether as a quiet celebration or a war song. Only LIVE. That is all that was ever asked of you. It is all you have ever had to give.

You are not immortal.

And this, too, is a gift.

Baking Banana Bread as the World Ends

These are things I have not noticed in a while.
The way the sun shines through the kitchen window
after furious thunder and lightning, little dancing droplets
    make small rainbows.

How the fragrance of a watery world,
softened soil and sky water, is lifted by the breeze
so it can meet me at the open window.

This world is a different realm now.
And I am a new survival,
aggressively hopeful and kind,

baking for the people I love,
pretending good cheer to keep the smiles going.
I thought the apocalypse would be a loud,

angry, breathless thing.
Instead, it sits with me on the porch,
fresh-baked banana bread crumbling

from its fingers and mine,
looking out quietly at the sparkling rainwater driveway
while I post glittery happy pictures on Twitter about what
    I will eat for dinner.

Notes on Survival

You are allowed to break.
Everything does.
The stars grow tired and fall.
The waves crash against rocks and shores.
Trees fall for both storms and wind
leaving behind seeds and saplings
so a version of them may grow again.
Storm clouds part for rain
then part for the sun to come through.
Night must break for day
and day for night in a cycle.
The world is made of broken things
piecing themselves back together
—this is what gives us the most resilient stories.
So why do you think that you were made
any differently than the night and the storm clouds?
You know how to put yourself back together again, too,
just as well as they do.

Take heart that you have managed
to rebuild yourself a thousand times
after every bad day.

That is no small thing.

A *Reminder from the Stars*

Constellations of stars exploded
to bring you to life.

The molecules in your left collarbone
come from a different galaxy than your right.

And by defiantly existing against all odds
you are honoring their sacrifice.

The Confrontation

This year has forced me to confront myself,
Everything that felt like a door closing made me realize
How many doors have been open;
I simply haven't walked through them.

All this ugliness I ignored,
All these wounds I refused to let heal
Because I found the pain more comfortable
Than letting go of what I knew.

This is what loneliness does.
It acts as a mirror for who you are.
And if you do not like it,
It gives you the time to change.

Loneliness says, "Peace is a thing of the imagination,
An invention you must picture to walk toward."
Loneliness says, "Whatever peace looks like, it is yours.
Yours to find. Yours to keep. Yours to cherish."

Small

(For S, *who still loves hard*)

Do you remember what
we called a crisis before this?

I remember a head full of overdue bills
and a broken-down car,

a house with no heating,
the bathroom shower always leaking,

arguing over messy housemates
who moved significant others in

and hoped we wouldn't notice,
or the time I refused to apologize

because I didn't want to admit I was wrong.
And now it all seems so insignificant,

so petty, so short-sightedly human.
I should have pulled you close that night,

run my fingers through the constellations
in your hair, and said, I *am so sorry*

that I am smaller and more selfish
than the warm, merciful love you need me to be.

On Raising Children During COVID-19

You cannot protect children by lying to them.
You cannot craft castles in the sky
and tell them this is what they're walking into,

press the bones of fairy tales into their minds
and hope for the best when the reality is
that lying politicians with careless policies

target those who are ill and have vulnerabilities.
How they are packed in classrooms despite their fears,
and are locked into their dorms despite their lonely tears.

There is no way to hide a cannibalistic planet
from innocent eyes, and believe me I have tried.
I have tried reading stories of sleeping princesses

and flying carpets, drowned darker news
in sugary-sweet voices, given them poetry,
but life is now perpetually prosaic.

I know now that to protect them is to tell them truths.
Speak of the lies and evil out there but also
teach that inside them is a warrior made of exactitude.

"Mother" has many avatars, but in this era,
she becomes sensei, too. Raising children
to strengthen themselves from the inside

by showing them how to defeat their worst fears,
by facing all their worst wounds,
fearless carved into their souls,

as they stare at a world that is a barren field,
and respond, *There is still something lovely here,*
under this hard ground. Faith waiting to be grown.

The Present

As I was sad today, I went out walking again.
And some people will say that isn't poem-worthy.
But poetry lives in everything ordinary
even walks where you pretend the trees are your family.

And though it was cold,
I bought some strawberry ice cream.
I also sang back at a blackbird's scream
while an old man laughed delightedly and called me crazy.

I stopped at the corner park
to watch autumn's first call,
as a show of ochre and amber
and flame leaves danced and fell.

On the way back home,
I thought of all these little happenings
and how well they helped me survive.
Despite anguish-ridden bones, I returned home feeling most
    alive.

In Contemplation

If there is anything I remember,
it is all the promises to friends I did not keep.

The coffee dates I didn't make,
the wine I didn't drink because I feared headaches,

the walks I should have taken
or the days I should have taken the later train.

And the stories we left unfinished.
Most of all, the conversations we never had.

If I had a chance to do it all over,
I would spend longer holding their hands,

even through our worst fights,
when emotion makes our voices shake,

and after, go for a walk so we can watch the mist rise over
    the waters,
on a cold evening as we walk by the lake.

Spring Cleaning

Throw away the knife you made from the sharp insults they gave you. Empty out the darkness that has accumulated at the bottom of your heart, all the words you refuse to say. Your heart is not a well to poison; remember that. When the secrets become too heavy to carry, whisper them to the wind to be whisked away.

As much as people say, "You do not have to do this alone," know that there are some things you must do alone—like find each part of you that no one has known how to love, hold it as it cries, and love it anyway.

Burn every memory that does not help you grow. Destruction, too, can be necessary. When you emerge from the burning, covered in the ashes of the person you once were, think of how even the most devastating wildfires burn away debris and nourish the soil so that new trees can grow.

Is a Poet Still a Poet in Quarantine?

It's midnight and I'm talking to the fridge again.
It never responds, only listens.

This house is not haunted
by anything except me.

I am the still-human ghost
that wanders between the rooms,

leaving traces of my humanness
to remind myself I am still alive.

Half a cup of now-cold tea.
Laundry waiting to be done.

I envy how the dust collects,
so I leave fingerprints on dusty shelves.

I apologize to the inanimate objects I bump into
like drunks do when they come home too late.

I ask myself, *Can writers even be lonely?*
We are used to inventing people out of thin air.

I have no excuse for being this way.
Other than the plague. And quarantine.

And all the other old-new words
we have had to become familiar with this year.

Sometimes I try to write a poem,
still trying to chase immortality.

But the poem asks, If a poet writes a poem
that no one ever reads, is she still a poet?

And I think, She is. She is still a poet,
the same way a tree is still a tree

when it falls alone in the forest.
It does make a sound.

But just like the tree,
she was there for a moment.

And then she is vanished by nature
as though she was never there at all.

Affirmation for Living On

You are still here.
Despite what time tells you.
Despite the loneliness.
Despite the darkness.
Despite the pain.
Despite the gritted teeth
and drowning thoughts.
You are still here.
And that *matters*
more than you know.

The Dynamics of Lonely

On a midnight walk,
in a forest full of stars,
I reconsider the way
lonely works.

How it gets into the bones
of children who grow to be
adults with abandonment issues
because of an absent parent.

How it hardens
the hearts of people
who use it to block
someone out of a group.

How the cruelest places
use lonely
as a punishment through
solitary confinement.

And how we spend our days
watching clocks in forlorn buildings,
waiting for when we can go home
to the warmth of love.

All this to divide us and conquer.
A wolf left alone in the wild
is easy prey, too.
That's why wolves live in packs.

They know that community
keeps every wolf healthier and safer,
each one fulfilling a duty to the other,
protecting and nurturing their young to be better.

Our strength then lies in numbers.
We are wildflowers, designed
to weather storms and grow in places
no one expects us, rising and thriving together.

2020 Redux

The year of *this is SO my year.*
The year of canceled plans and tears.
The year of working from home but living at work.
The year of I *suppose lockdown has some perks.*
The year of fires first, answers later.
The year of sourdough bread and no toilet paper.
The year of queuing and fevers.
The year the apocalypse told us stories instead,
and death came to live next door.
The year of breakups and breakdowns.
The year of *anxiety is my new best friend.*
The year of *when we see each other again.*
The year of death without goodbyes.
The year of *if we see each other again.*
The year of *optimism is a destination so far away.*
The year of *you owe it to yourself to live through it all anyway.*

Red Giant
noun

- ASTRONOMY
  A very large star of high luminosity and low surface tempera-ture. Red giants are thought to be in a late stage of evolution when no hydrogen remains in the core to fuel nuclear fusion.

- INFORMAL
  The stage in which a star is holding on to its life as fiercely as it can.

When the Crisis Hit

All I could do was worry.
Panic sat inside my body,
a withering wrenching
that refused to go away.

I thought of all the things
I had left unfinished.
All the wrongs I had not righted.
All the relationships I had not mended.

Outside the storm continued heavy and unforgiving.
I sat indoors fretting, biting my nails.
Outside the squirrel buries her acorn
and will soon forget about it,

while I wonder how I have carried so many regrets
without even realizing they were there.
And it occurred to me that I, too,
knew how to bury and forget.

So instead I took my worries out
and laid them carefully on the kitchen table.
Then began the slow but rewarding task
of fixing everything that needed more love.

Picking up each worry
and examining it closely,
honoring it with the time it needed
that I never had to give it before.

In Isolation

We think of everything
we can still rely on.

The moon.
Except on a cloudy day.

The clouds.
*But they are in a rush
and never stop to greet us on the way.*

The trees, at least, are a certainty.
*Except for when the wind knocks them down
with its forceful intensity.*

The sun is a constant then.
*Except when the sky
fills with clouds again.*

The little stream in the woods, though?
*It evaporates during the summer,
didn't you know?*

And what of the stars that still shine every night?
*They are long dead, and have been
for as long as we have known this life.*

The rivers, the seas, the oceans, too?
*Constantly changing,
like me and you.*

So what do we have to rely on then?

How do we find certainty again?
Maybe the answer is
we never had it at all.

That life never promised us constants,
but just the same chance it offers
everything we know.

To change and live and breathe
to the fullest we can
and in the best way we know how.

The Fawn

(*After Mary Oliver's "Wild Geese"*)

You do not have to win at a crisis.
You do not have to push yourself
to learn a new language or write a book
or take up an instrument.
Nothing will come of forcing yourself
to compete your way out of trauma.
Take this time to look at the stars.
Take this time to look at how the sky
still holds clouds that are the shape of hope.
How the dawn begins at the tips of dewy grass,
for this is where the horizon begins.
Somewhere the dappled fawn raises
her soft neck to watch the sun rise
over her meadow.
Somewhere else monarch butterflies begin
their long migration, knowing many of them
will not make it home.
Remember that you do not need to earn
your right to the precious minutes you have
on this planet. They are already yours,
like the fawn and the butterflies.
The universe beckons you to enjoy this life
it has given you through a heart
that beats to the rhythm of
its very own cosmic song.

Affirmation for Days of Self-Loathing

On the days you find the mirror hard to look at,
remember there is a myth which says

the face you have in this life
is the face of the person you loved most

in your last.
I know it's just a myth.

But think of how much more love
you would give yourself if it were true.

Across

Across the shooting stars and galaxies / across black holes and all mad, sad things / across the joyful laughter of new parents / and the tragedy of losing someone you love / across the oceans with their sharks and secrets / and across an atmosphere both full of satellites and full of spacedust / across the devastation of a world that has known trauma better than it has known healing for too long / across the silence that brings pain and the songs that ease hearts / across the knowing and unknowing of all things / across depression, anxiety, and panic, too / across the people we once loved and the people we will love / you were made for fiercer, better things / and I promise this grief, too, is only fleeting.

A Reminder from Smaller Beings

The bird building her home on your windowsill
has had every nest destroyed before.

The spider that is delicately weaving a silken masterpiece
has had every single thread broken before.

And despite it all,
they try again.

A Lesson on Love

My dog and I do not speak the same language.
Yet every day, she tells me:
I *trust you to know when I need to go for a walk.*
I *will let you hold me when you need to*
and I will ask you for love when I need it.
On *the days you are sick, I will lie beside you.*
I *will look for you in rooms when you are not here,*
and I will greet you with so much joy
when you come home.
I *will guard you when you sleep.*
I *will wag my tail and let you know*
that everything will be okay
on your bad days,
and I know that you will do
the same on mine.

And from this I learn that my dog
and I actually do speak the same language.

After all, the universe is a kindly ancient thing.
It gave love as a mother tongue to every being.

Good Blood

My mother never says goodbye. Instead she says, *Be kind*. And by this she means, sometimes, pay for someone's coffee behind you in line. When a small boy drops his bag of oranges on the train, help him pick them up. Hold the door open for the old lady with a walking stick. And offer the tired nurse your seat on the Underground. And by this she means, say *thank you* a little more. Give smiles away for free, even if you get none back or they may not be seen because of your mask. Listen with an open heart to everyone's stories. Let the person behind you in line go first. Buy lunch for someone without a home who you see on the street. Grab the thing off the top shelf for someone who is struggling to reach. And by this she means, we must strive to give little joys to each other's spirits now. Little compassions in a life that is hard for us all somehow. If it is hate that divides us, then perhaps this is where we rake our fingers through the dirt of these borders, and how we can build these sacred bonds again.

When my mother says, *Be kind*, she means, *There is too much bad blood between us all. Leave some good blood instead.*

How to Deal with a Painful Experience

Let it hurt,
let it bleed,
let it heal,
and then, let it go.

Reminder for Days of Uncertainty

You cannot mourn the life
you haven't lived yet,
only one that has already gone.

You will never know the meadows
you could grow, if you are fixated
on the ashes of a garden you never had.

Abundance

My grandfather, with his bronzed hands
full of dark soil from planting dahlias,
tells me to focus on the bounty
we have been given:

A sky so wide and full
that it carries every color
of blue and pink and orange
you can imagine.

And a sun that warms us
from our head to our toes,
and gives us reason sometimes to say,
Beautiful weather today!

And a moon so gentle
that she even wins the stormy seas over
and gives us a beauty to gaze at
in the arms of our lovers.

And a planet of such abundance
that it gives us so much nourishment;
shade in the form of trees,
flowers that glow radiant for our eyes to see.

So do not despair at all your falls.
There is still happiness
to be had here,
no matter how small.

An example, my grandfather says,
while looking at my grandmother,
is that with just a good heart and some tenderness,
you, too, can have a love that lasts lifetimes.

What If

What if this is all there is?
What if the sickness is permanent?
What if we run out of food and water?
What if we fall so hard we can't get back up?
What if we forget how to breathe?
What if all our stories have sad endings?
What if the night falls out of love with the day?
What if winter never leaves?
What if the sky decides it has had enough?
What if the earth gets bored of its orbit?
What if the sun becomes a black hole?
What if it swallows our solar system?
What if this is how it all ends?

Then the stardust that makes me
will still find the stardust makes you,
and together we will find a home again.

Daily Mantra 3

Things must fall to pieces,
diminish into dust, ashes to ashes,
before they pull themselves together
reassemble, reboot.
I mean, the world.
I mean, you.

The Last Rose of the Season

In the moments life feels like an empty word,
And my bones feel more burdens than they can bear,

I think of the last coral rose in my garden,
Holding on despite all her sisters

In decaying petals on the same soil
She has risen from.

Every day, despite frost and fog,
She stays, as if to ask me,

"Do you love life enough?
Do you hold it with both fury and tenderness?

Do you understand its fleeting nature
Or do you resent its darknesses

Forgetting to live
Because the pain is too strong

Or the tests too tedious and long?
Do you understand, for you, winter's biting cold

Will always be followed by spring's flourish
And summer's honeyed warmth?

I only get to live for a season,
But you get so much more,

So live, live, live,
Because I cannot."

In those moments, I thank her for her lessons
And tend to her gently,

Hoping for a miracle that
She lives through winter to enjoy spring again.

Essential

My nephew is six. All big brown eyes
and full of bright, shining curiosity.

His mother is a nurse.
An essential worker.

We are eating jam sandwiches
near the small pond in the park,

close to the water's edge, when he asks,
But are we not essent-shual workers?

I nod somberly. *No, we are not,
for you are a small boy and I am a poet.*

He ponders this as he wipes
sticky strawberry hands on the grass.

What does my mum do?
he asks finally.

She saves lives,
I say.

Can I save lives?
a small catch in his little voice,

and I am about to say,
Maybe one day.

But his attention is caught by something
disturbing the peaceful waters of the pond.

A large ant. Its legs move frantically as it drowns.
My nephew takes the small discarded package,

empty now of our sandwiches,
and turns it into a bridge for the ant.

The ant makes its way onto the paper,
and scurries off into the grass.

And from this I learned
that ants deserve to live as much as we do,

that sometimes paper can become a bridge,
and the smallest of beings can save the littlest lives, too.

Listening to the Rain at the End of the World

And I realize no one has told it,
pattering on my window
as though it is knocking to get in,

that the world is coming to an end.
No one told the flowers in the garden
or the trees in the woods.

No one told the dandelions on the hill
where we walk the dog or the birds
that nest on the window in the shed.

So I go outside to tell the rain
the flowers the trees the dandelions the birds
and they laugh and whisper soothingly,

We have been at this same end
countless times before.
But the earth is ancient enough

to know how to
reincarnate
and begin again.

People-Shaped Universes

Someone once told me,
We are the universe expressing itself
as a human for a while.

It makes me think
of every person I meet
as their own little universe,

each with their own planets of thoughts
and solar systems of dreams
and galaxies of emotions in their bloodstreams.

People are so much bigger
on the inside than they seem
on the outside.

Imagine a whole world
of universes constantly
bumping into each other,

listening and learning
and sometimes,
just sometimes,

building a perishable forever together.

Main Sequence (Resilience)
noun

- ASTRONOMY
  Any star that is fusing hydrogen in its core and has a stable balance of outward pressure. Ninety percent of the stars in the universe, including our sun, are main sequence stars.

- INFORMAL
  The stage during which a star is happiest and most stable.

More Reasons to Stay

In a multiverse full of infinite possibilities,
you only get one chance to love the people you have loved,
to be full of joy for the happiness that has walked your way,
to know the things that still amaze you every day,
to witness that sunset that changed you forever,
to stand before a view so stunning you'll never forget it,
to know the people who are still here despite it all.

Imagine how much more there is still to see.

Stay.
Stay.
Stay.

How to Be Strong

There are no rules.
You are already strong.

Even when you fall apart
in the most public place you know.

Even when your knees hit the floor
and your trauma meets you in floods.

Even when your body wracks with sobs
fashioned in the belly of a tsunami.

Even when the sorrow feels like
the endless nature of drowning,

your grit is right there
inside you.

Your strength is within you always
to call up when you want to.

And besides, didn't anyone ever tell you
that endurance, that resilience,

that *strength* looks
so different on us all?

On some it looks like still waters and on others
it looks like a dam bursting as the water falls.

Lessons for Future Selves

What doesn't kill you gives you trauma.
Time steals memories; it doesn't heal wounds.
Nothing's fair in love, war, life, or living.
It doesn't pass; you learn to live with it.
When life gives you lemons,
hand them back and ask for flour
you can make a cake out of.
Mostly what glitters is kindness, not gold,
and you should use it everywhere:
the world needs more shine.
Time isn't in the habit
of telling anyone anything.
It knows better than to get mixed up
with your messes.
Dance into love instead of falling
and dance back out of it grateful.
Drown in happiness instead of sorrow.
Everything is too perishable to last eternities.
Build your own blisses.
They will not last.
Celebrate each one anyway.

Daily Mantra 4

You are still here.
Still made of interstellar blood.
Still constellation skinned.
Still defying the world's endless trials.
Coping through every bad day.
That's all courage is in the end.
A reason to keep fighting.
Defying every odd to stay.

The Masterpiece

If all a lifetime must be
is the noise between
two silences,
then there is no reason
we cannot turn existence
into the most beautiful
masterpiece we ever make.
Let the sky feel like a symphony
God composed just for you.
Let the crimson roses
paint awake their brightest colors
all for you.
Let the grief
that is telling you stories
remember it is not invited to stay.
Let the love
you do not know how to give anymore
dance out of you another way.
Let every person on this planet
rise one morning and think,
What good can I do to nourish the soul?
Let there be joy
when we commemorate
the end of all things.
Let there be songs
as we see the endings
are only beginnings.

The Making of You

The universe had to fall apart into dust first
to become its majestic, infinite self.
What makes you think
this trauma, this devastation,
won't be the making of
a more powerful you, too?

Kindness and Hate Meet for a Drink at the End of the World

They do it because their mother dislikes
how uncomfortable Sunday lunches have become.
Politics shouldn't affect us this much.
She insists, *Family finds ways to make things work.*

Mum, please.
The apocalypse is his fault,
Kindness tries to explain.
But her mum is having none of it.

So Kindness, ever the dutiful daughter, sighs and agrees.
Even though she knows well enough
how uncordial Hate is going to be.
Their mother says, *It's just what he's made of.*

And Kindness is expected to understand,
she is always expected to understand.
So she arrives early at the pub
to work out their differences.

Hate is loud and late as always.
She hears him come in, fists clenched,
knocking over glasses at full tables
and breaking things just because he can.

She watches as he grins at the chaos,
causes an argument between a son and his father
who seemed happy a few minutes ago.
Thrives on the pain.

By the time he reaches her,
Hate has destroyed the jovial spirit in the pub.
Kindness makes eye contact with him,
smiles gently in greeting but walks past him,

goes to help pick the glasses up.
Calms down their tired nerves.
Helps rebuild what is broken.
Puts a calming hand on the father and son to stop their
    fighting.

Kindness gets under Hate's skin.
Rage fills him as she walks back to him.
She buys pints for them both as he sneers and says,
You are such a bleeding heart.

Kindness shrugs, I *just care.*
He laughs. *Why? What's the point?*
She looks at him carefully.
Community. Civic duty. Being good—

All of which is boring, he interrupts rudely.
Maybe to you, she says. *But to me, it fixes the world.*
Hate bursts out laughing.
You? Fix the world? NEVER.

Selfishness and Cruelty never did either,
she says patiently, trying to be better,
but Hate simply spits in her direction,
says, *Get over it. The world is mine now, you lost.*

Without another word, he leaves.
And Kindness doesn't know if she can save the world.
But she is small, and dedicated,
and she has Hope and Courage and Love by her side.

So she gets up and pays for her drinks
and promises Hate's retreating back,
I will *fix the world no matter how loud you are.*
I *will try and try and try.*

More Notes on Survival

Someone is talking to me
about the light at the end of the tunnel
and all I can think of is *after*.
What happens after we meet the light.
After the grief ends.
After we walk into happiness.
Won't there be another tunnel,
another painful passage,
another trauma simply waiting?
And the answer is, *yes*,
because in the book of being,
life promised to be a moving thing.
It promised to be both fight and flourish.
It vowed to be both lesson and respite.
So the love will end.
The light will end.
The joy will end.
And as we keep walking,
we find it again.

Affirmations for Strength

There is nothing ugly about you.
Mistakes are a human rite of passage.
We all make them.

You put the forgiveness inside your chest.
Look for it in the first chamber of your heart.
It lives there for you, too. Do not forget that.

Other people cannot love the pain out of you.
The bright side is, you can learn
how to honor the pain so that you can welcome love in.

A clenched fist does not always have the answers.
Feel the breeze against your palm once in a while and allow the
    fight to be tomorrow's problem.

The world may seem like an ugly place right now,
but there is so much you do not know of it yet,
and a lot of what you do not know is exquisite.

Prayer in Lockdown

Some mornings, the weight of your sadnesses will be too heavy for you to get out of bed. Some afternoons will be spent in the arms of sorrow instead of tenacity. Some midnights you will remember every mistake you ever made, try to hold yourself together, and fail. This is shattering. This is coming undone in the most brutal ways possible. You are suddenly a void. You feel like an empty planet battling your own core. A war is still a war even if it is inside your head, did you know this? A wound left unhealed is bound to open again. That's just what being human *is*. Fearless has always grown best in unknowing hands. That is what fearless *is*. Not knowing what is going to happen next and facing it anyway. Reminding yourself at the end that you are worth saving. When the pieces of you spill out of your hands, picking them up once again. And perhaps today is not the day that you face the harrowing. Perhaps today you just sit there, on the floor, counting the broken pieces of yourself.

This is still prayer.
You are still sacred.
Some days, this is what holy will look like.
How you resurrect yourself again.

Progress

The bad news is,
what was shattered
may never be possible to rebuild.

The good news is,
what you make in its place
will be better than what was destroyed.

The Recipe

It is never too late to find passion for your purpose again.

All you have to do is pluck your worst fears out and put them
into a cauldron, sprinkle in some crimson love to sweeten,
pick fresh green sprigs of determination from the plant you
so lovingly grew in the garden of your heart.

Mix it all up and then take a generous tablespoon of golden
forgiveness, and this part is important: allow it to boil, then
simmer.

We aren't making just any recipe. We are reigniting your
passion for living, and that is an arduous task. So, be brave
and patient. When it is ready, you will know.

You will also know to pluck some leaves of wild hope growing
by your kitchen window, mix it into the golden green swirls
that look like a delicious story waiting to be told.

You don't need to drink this all at once.

Instead, drain it into a jar and keep it in your fridge.

Pour yourself a cup when the world tries to take from you what
you love most.

Drink it when they tell you that you have no fire, when you
feel your existence was a mistake.

Drink it and tell yourself the fire is there, it just needs a spark.
That you have every right to be here, holding this difficult
life carefully in your hands and turning living into a fine art.

How to Be Happy Again

The wretchedness will come like a raven wishing to be fed.
Do not reject it.

The sorrow will coil up like a poem your fingers refuse to
    write.
Do not turn this anguish away.

The fears will talk over each other while caught in your throat.
Slowly untangle them and let them sit with you anyway.

Despite what they tell you,
it's okay.

It's okay to feel small and alone sometimes.
It's okay to feel like a lonely cottage in the clouds,

like you are all alone in your great big feelings,
all these painful things that break you.

Brave faces are just that,
faces *trying* to look brave.

Toxic positivity is just that.
Positivity trying so hard it's turning into poison.

Healing is just a mess demanding to be felt.
Especially the things we wish we didn't have to feel.

So feed the wretchedness.
Feel the anguish and write the poem.

Invite the fears to explain themselves till they are tired.
And when everything has been fed and felt and has exhausted
    itself,

give yourself the permission,
the space, to be happy,

even if the happiness
has not found its way back to you yet.

Hymn for the Future

May you always know pain
as temporary and laughter better.

May the universe bless you
with the perseverance to try harder.

May you build a kinder history
than the ruins that you were given.

May the greatest gift you receive be more
than just a life, but a life where the air is safer,

a life so full of love and joy
that it is worth living.

And Even Through This

Someone fell in love today.
Someone was born today.
Someone lived through something
that could have killed them.
Someone won back the love of their life.
Someone made their parents proud.
Someone survived.
Someone healed.
Someone let go.

Seven billion people,
and some have just had the best day
of their lives.

Today may have been
the very worst day of yours.

But take solace
and celebrate this simple fact.

It wasn't your best day today,
but it is on its way,
because we all get lucky in turn.

Silver Linings

When uncertainty sends your spirit declining,
and anxiety becomes as familiar as your own name,
pause, breathe, let me show you some silver linings.

They say that the swans have returned to Venice
and the waters have become clear again.
They say you can finally see blue skies in cities again.

Who knew that social isolation could bring people closer?
We see Italians sing and dance together on their balconies,
people finally calling up to check on their neighbors.

And may we never take meeting each other
for granted ever again, and may we realize
compassion is all that makes this life worth living.

So especially when it feels like the end now,
we must remember that an ending is the start
of another beautiful something,

that there is *always* light to be had at the end of grieving.

Nebula (Rebirth)
noun

- ASTRONOMY
  A cloud of dust particles, hydrogen, helium, and other vapors in the cosmos, sometimes visible as a bright patch.

- INFORMAL
  A place where stars are born.

Catching the Light

It'll hide from you.
Secrete itself away
inside experiences and people.

You'll find it in unusual places,
like a small child's song
and a grandmother's smile.

Kindness always brings it out.
As does the courage to do the right thing,
despite the cruelty trying to tear you apart.

It'll glow through the darkest days,
and that's how you catch it
inside the pocket of your heart.

The Oak

In the poetry of existence,
the oak tree stands tall,

despite the winds that try
to knock it down.

The grass grows again,
even if it is cut every two weeks.

The stars shine, defying
their own deaths across time.

The birds migrate across a sky
that promises heavy storms.

And the leaves shed at autumn
and sprout again at spring.

All of this says,
if brave was easy,

it would not belong
in this family.

It is in our DNA, our bones.
We all have it in us to be heroes.

Daily Mantra 5

There is no better time
to learn how to love yourself
than the mirror that silence gives you.
This is the time to reflect on all those things
about yourself that no one has ever
taught you how to love.

The Forest

One day, when you wake up,
you will find that you've become a forest.

You've grown roots and found strength in them
that no one thought you had.

You have become stronger
and full of life-giving qualities.

You have learned to take all the negativity around you
and turn it into oxygen for easy breathing.

A host of wild creatures live inside you
and you call them stories.

A variety of beautiful birds nest inside your mind
and you call them memories.

You have become an incredible
self-sustaining thing of epic proportions.

And you should be so proud of yourself,
of how far you have come from the seeds of who you used
    to be.

What They Do Not Tell You About Miracles

Is how they come from complete chaos.
How everything around us *must* fall apart
before we can make something better.

How the veil of comfort must be ripped
from our faces for us to be able to truly grow.
This is what the stars, the sun, and the moon already know.

Here are the parts of what makes a successful miracle.
Let healing arrive where there is agony.
Let beauty rise where there is tragedy.

Let joy fill up spaces and defeat violence.
Let it be followed by benevolence.
May everything good thrive despite this ruthlessness.

Your Soft Heart

You are still the child who gently places
Fallen baby birds back in their nests.
You are still the soft soul that gets
Your heart broken over cruel words
And awful acts when you watch the news.
You are still the gentle heart who once
Tried to heal a flower by attempting to stick
Its petals back on when ignorant feet trampled it.

This is why you are important.
This is why you will always be needed.

Kindness is the greatest endangered thing.
And here you are, existing, your heart so full with it.

Kindness

And maybe it is easier to learn kindness in these times.
When the whole world is like a small child with a fever,
trying her very best to make herself feel better.

Maybe we find our unity in the near losing of everything.
Where we have no choice but to depend upon each other—
    key workers, volunteers, and neighbors.
This is what it takes to realize we are in this together.

A man helps someone he dislikes because they are in danger.
A neighbor delivers groceries to everyone ill on her street.
Old friends forgive each other and stop acting like they are
    strangers.

Maybe this time, this is when the revolution arrives dressed
    as kindness.
People helping each other despite their differences.
Understanding, truly, that without the aid of others

we would be all alone in this.

Love in the Time of Coronavirus

(For Trista Mateer)

Today, we stockpile empathy.
We supply love and good energy.
We sing to each other across buildings.
We say I *love you* through social distancing.

Do you know that writing letters
to our friends is back in fashion?
And that we finally have time to read more books,
whether historical or fiction?

My cousin told me she hadn't seen
such a blue sky in her city before.
My uncle went on his first walk in the woods.
He heard a bird sing for the first time since he went to war.

Even in sickness, this world
is allowed to be beautiful.
And we are still allowed to love it,
for there is always room for hope.

This is just me checking in,
sending you the moon as a poem,
praying and wishing for us all
a speedy recovery.

And if nothing else,
there will always be poetry.
We will always have poetry.

Cities, Ruins, and You

New York City was partly built from the wartime ruins
of English cathedrals, and libraries, and homes.

Rome was created again from what was left of it
after it had burned to nothing but ashes.

New Delhi is still standing, a gorgeous amalgamation
of old and new history after thousands of years of war.

And these are simply
>   *cities.*

So what makes you believe that you,
with the healing force

of the whole universe behind you,
cannot rebuild your heart,

cannot rise like a phoenix from the ashes
that were left of you?

How can you possibly believe
that these ruins are the end of you?

93 Percent Stardust
(*After Carl Sagan, who gave me hope as a child*)

We have calcium in our bones,
iron in our veins,
carbon in our souls,
and nitrogen in our brains.

93 percent stardust,
with souls made of flames,
we are all just stars
that have people names.

Daily Mantra 6

Beauty exists alongside the ugliness.
The dark side of the moon doesn't destroy its shine.
The stars are both common and rare.
The world is not an either, an or, but both,
And every quiet, bright shade in between.
On the days you are hardest on yourself,
Remember you are a child of this universe,
That you too contain all the little infinities
As a human just trying to be.

Where Hope Comes From

It comes from heartache.
And it grows like the lone sapling
from the ashes of loss.
And it carves its way out
of the heavy heart of tragedy and its heavy cost.
And it rises like a soldier, thought lost,
returning home to his mother.
And it smiles like the calm, clear sky
following weeks of one storm after another.

And maybe this is why, when Pandora
opened the box that carried such calamities,
which afflicted all of mankind,
gentle hope emerged from there, too.

What else helps us
overcome suffering
if not giving hope
a chance to bloom?

Acknowledgments

My beautiful family. Though we are far apart, I hope to see you soon.

My lovely agent Niki Chang, who has been so supportive and brilliant to me always.

The wonderful Sam Eades, for being an excellent editor and pushing me to do my best.

Trista, for being one of the first people to look at these poems and guide me.

Steve, for being so amazing through this process.

Nikesh, for always being there for me. Thank you, my brother.

Susannah, Gaby, Sim, for being a constant source of positivity and poetry in a heartbreaking time.

Nerm, Anoushka, Salena, Nadine, Safiya, Joelle, Carlos, Roger, Roshni, Sunnah, Sheena, Sharan, Sophia, Sanah, Dean, Pragya, for being powerful creatives and inspirations.

Ewoma, Emma, Lauz, Clare, Layla, Alison, Shaun, Rebekah, Clara, Annie, Dave, Heather, Matt, Faye, Iain, for your support and love.

And finally, thank you to you, dear reader. May you always find what you're looking for.

With verse, warmth, and love,
Nikita

ALSO AVAILABLE
FROM NIKITA GILL

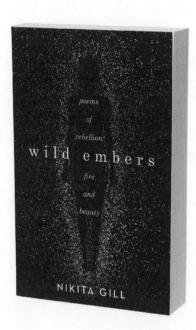

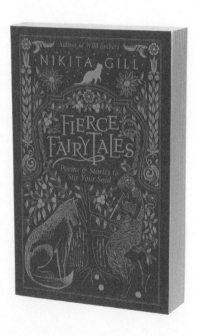